Suzhou–the paradise on earth.

人 间 天 堂

苏 州

苏州市旅游局 · 中国旅游出版社 编辑

中国旅游出版社

编　　辑：苏州市旅游管理局
　　　　　中国旅游出版社
主　　编：韩先云
责任编辑：龚威健　蔡盘麟
图片编辑：陈健行　周仁德　郑　翔
撰　　文：朱熙均
翻　　译：沈仲辉　赵信华
装帧设计：龚威健　陈晓冰
篆　　刻：蔡廷辉
地图绘制：田　静
摄　　影：(按姓氏笔划为序)
　　　　　丁　虹　朱熙均　毕晓华　印祖庆　孙凤初
　　　　　孙健平　许树东　刘智常　张尧俊　张丽娜
　　　　　沈锦伟　张家振　陈健行　陈　峥　吴万一
　　　　　周仁德　周纯炎　周春燕　金勤淳　茅　红
　　　　　闻　军　查正风　郑　翔　翁兰青　顾春军
　　　　　唐嘉鸿　龚威健　黄铭杰　韩先云　谢新发
　　　　　阙瑞明

图书在版编目（CIP）数据

苏州／韩先云主编. —北京：中国旅游出版社，
2001.3
ISBN 7-5032-1818-5

Ⅰ.苏… Ⅱ.韩… Ⅲ.名胜古迹－苏州市－图集
Ⅳ.K928.705.33-64

中国版本图书馆 CIP 数据核字（2001）第 11273 号

苏　州

出版发行：中国旅游出版社
地　　址：北京建国门内大街甲九号
邮政编码：100005
电　　话：010 — 65201174
制　　版：深圳利丰雅高电分制版有限公司
印　　刷：东莞新扬印刷有限公司
版　　次：2001 年 3 月第 1 版
印　　次：2002 年第 1 版第 2 次
开　　本：850 × 1168 毫米　　1/24
印　　张：4　　　（005800）

苏州市在中国地图上的位置
The Location of Suzhou
on the Map of China

北京市 Beijing

中 华 人 民 共 和 国
People's Republic of China

江苏省
JIANGSU

苏州市
Suzhou

南海诸岛

封面：虎丘雪景(摄影：陈建行)
Huqiu covered with snow.

封底：江南水乡—周庄(摄影：印祖庆)。
Zhouzhuang-a renowned village in South China.

目
录
CONTENTS

前　言
Foreword

有学者说：城市是文化的容器。

苏州，这座文化容器，像人类遗迹的文化堆积层。从它的剖面来看，每层都有丰富多彩的内容，读之不尽。

从它的宏观来看，有文人将苏州城概括为：鱼米之乡、园林之城、锦绣之市、文物之邦。

鱼米之乡，靠的是地理优势，太湖、大运河在旁，气候温和，土地肥沃，再加上历史的赐予。六千年以前世界上还少有种水稻时，苏州的老祖宗就种植水稻。时空让苏州的农民悠悠地精耕细作。

园林，是苏州的文化结晶，早在晋代就有士大夫建造私家园林，以求"不出城廓而有山水之乐"。历来，富贵人家有园林，平头百姓也有天井、庭院，包括还有缩小了的园林——苏派盆景艺术。

锦绣之市，说的是13世纪，苏州出产的丝绸锦缎，就名扬中外了。以后，苏州又是江南丝绸工业的中心之一。所谓"日出万匹，衣被天下"。

苏州刺绣最早见于宋代（虎丘塔出土的经袱绣品）。苏绣以样纹秀丽，针法多样见称，绣品精巧典雅，而与湘绣、粤绣、蜀绣共誉为中国四大名绣。

所谓文物之邦，说的是这里有文化古迹，有人文故事、传说。人文荟萃之地，就必然萌生流派，有文学的、有画坛的、

有音乐的(包括昆曲、评弹)，而且在中国文化艺术史上占有一定的地位。

这里有众多的博物馆，除了综合性的博物馆以外，还有丝绸博物馆、刺绣博物馆、戏曲博物馆、民俗博物馆、钱币博物馆，等等。

如果容许夸张的话，苏州城本身就是座古塔博物馆，有七塔八幢之说；也可说是座桥梁博物馆。马可·波罗说，有桥六千，那是以讹传讹。按平江图上看，有桥314座，直到现在古城区内有桥161座，连同城外一百多座，苏州市区有三百多座桥梁。

生活在这样一座城市里，感觉如何？

借用马可·波罗的说法：此城名苏州，法兰西语犹言"地"，而其近一别城行在(注：杭州)，则犹言"天"。因其繁华，故有是名。

其实，早在宋代就有"上有天堂，下有苏杭"之说。而这位外国老爷爷不谙汉语，有口难译，已说不清原话了。不能责怪老爷爷，只能带着微笑、拱手感谢他、尊敬他。他把苏州天堂之说传到了海外！

为方便"天堂之旅"，特编辑此画册，权充导游，但愿读者翻阅画册并亲临其境，体会苏州的历史文化韵味。

Some scholars say that the city is the container for culture.

The cultural container of Suzhou, like the sedimentation of the remains of human activities, shows variegated contents from its cross section.

In the larger sense, scholars have summarized the city as the "land of fish and rice", "city of gardens", "home of silk", and "metropolis of arts".

The "land of fish and rice" is based on the geographical position, the Lake Taihu, the Grand Canal passing by, the mild climate, fertile soil, and the traditions of agriculture. The forefathers of Suzhou began growing paddy rice some 6,000 years ago, when it was still a rarity in the world. The peasants of Suzhou have time and space at their disposal in meticulous tilling of the land.

The classical gardens are the crystallization of Suzhou culture. Officials back in the Jin Dynasty started building their private gardens "to enjoy the scenery of hills and waters without going out of town". In the various times, wealthy families owned their gardens, and ordinary homes had courtyards or small open courts, including the miniaturized gardens – the Suzhou-style potted landscapes.

The "home of silk" refers to the fact that Suzhou had become famous both in

China and abroad as early as the 13th century for its production of silks. Afterwards, it became the base of silk industry in the southern Yangtze delta, reputed for "ten thousand bolts of silk being woven daily and claimed by the whole country."

Suzhou embroidery, which first appeared in the Song Dynasty (evidenced by the embroidered wrappings for Buddhist scriptures unearthed from the Tiger Hill Pagoda) and noted for delicate, rich stitch varieties and elegant, exquisite craftsmanship, is one of the four great schools of Chinese embroidery, the other three being those of Hunan, Guangdong, and Sichuan.

The "metropolis of arts" refers to the cultural relics, tales and legends. In this cradle of men of letters, there are bound to be various schools of literature, painting, and music (including Kunqu Opera and Suzhou Ballad Singing), which constitute an important part of the history of Chinese culture and art.

There are all kinds of museums. Besides the comprehensive types, there are silk museum, embroidery art museum, theatrical art museum, folk custom museum, and coinage museum, etc.

It is little exaggeration that the city itself is a museum of ancient pagodas. A popular saying goes that there are seven pagodas and eight temples in the city. The city can also be called a museum of

bridges. Marco Polo reported 6,000 bridges in Suzhou. He was obviously misinformed. From Pingjiang Map of the Song Dynasty, 314 bridges are counted in town. Now 161 bridges have remained inside the city. Besides, there are over a hundred bridges in the suburbs.

How would one feel to live in a city like this?

Marco Polo is quoted as saying: The name of Suzhou means "earth" in French, while the name of another city nearby means "heaven"; both cities are famous for great prosperity.

A popular saying back in the Song Dynasty goes: "Paradise in heaven, Suzhou and Hangzhou on earth." His Lordship Marco Polo meant to interpret the saying, but owing to his insufficient knowledge of the Chinese language, did not convey the original meaning, and we certainly should not blame him. Instead, we respect him and thank him with a smile for introducing Suzhou overseas as an earthly paradise.

This photo album is compiled as a guide to the "paradise tour" in the hope of motivating the readers for a visit to Suzhou to get the authentic historical and cultural feel of the city.

1. 拙政园中部。
1. The central section of the Humble
   Administrator's Garden.

古典园林
The Classical Gardens

中国古典园林不同于欧洲的花园。

古典园林,有皇家苑囿(包括打猎、饲养珍禽异兽)和私家园林之分。

皇家苑囿,追求规模、气魄,甚至包括真山真水,建筑金碧辉煌,气势逼人。苏州园林,都是私家园林,追求小中见大,回复自然,以诗情画意取胜,是融合我国传统庭园建筑、名木花卉、湖石叠山、汇水成池,以及文学、绘画等意蕴的一门综合艺术。

造园艺术的理论起源于苏州。明代苏州吴江人计成著有《园冶》。这是造园的经典著作。

古典园林的建造和规划,往往有画家参与。如明代著名画家文徵明为拙政园的建造,作了设计规划。

古典园林造园的手法,通常有"景区分隔"、"借景"、"对比"、"虚实并举"等等,使园景千变万化,移步换景,似隔非隔,曲径通幽,并借助历代文人留下的艺术作品如匾额、抱柱、楹联、题咏、图画、碑刻,以及古代家具、室内陈设、建筑装饰等手段,深化人们对景色的理解。

古典园林都有上百年的古树,缺了古树就称不上古典园林。园林古树尤为珍贵。

古典园林的理论和构造,早在古代就传到日本、欧洲。18世纪,英国人钱易斯在中国生活过,回国后作专著介绍中国园林,因

而在英国、欧洲出现"英华花园",曾风靡一时。

古典园林是把大自然的山山水水浓缩在

咫尺的天地中。文学家形容说,苏州园林是一把绘有美妙图画的折扇。苏州人自己却习惯在家居的天井里制作一盆水石盆景,栽以青苔、小草,点缀小小的亭台、小桥和小船,俨然是更加缩小了的家庭园林。

苏州人真会白相,他们的情趣在营造花园。人最美好的东西的确是花园——天堂。

拙政园,是中国名园,水面较多,主要建筑临水而筑,配以平桥低栏和芦汀小岛,似

江南风光。

沧浪亭,是苏州最古老的园林,建于宋代。

苏州著名的园林,还有网师园、留园、狮子林、怡园、耦园、环秀山庄、艺圃等十来座园林。还有小到只有半型的"半园",所有亭、台、楼、阁都只有半片,水只有一汪、桥只有几步,显得尤为精致。

拙政园、留园、网师园、环秀山庄、沧浪亭、狮子林、艺圃、耦园、退思园,都被联合国教科文组织列为《世界文化遗产名录》。

别了园林,何时再逢,留有图片,相寻梦里。

The Chinese classical gardens are distinctly different from those of Europe.

The classical gardens falls into two major categories: the royal gardens (including the game park for hunting and raising of games and fowls), and the private gardens.

The royal gardens are designed in huge dimensions and scales, often involving natural mountains and waters, with gorgeous, stately buildings.

Suzhou gardens belong to the private type of gardens. The book "Creation of Gardens" by Ji Cheng, a native of Wujiang, Suzhou, in the Ming Dynasty, is the classic work on landscape gardens.

The creation of classical gardens was often participated by artists. Wen Zhenming, a great painter of the Ming, for example, offered planning ideas for the construction of the Humble Administrator's Garden.

3

The frequently applied techniques in classical gardening, the "division of landscape areas", "borrowed views", "contrasting scenes", and "combination of the real with illusion", etc., achieve the effect of varied prospects that change with every step in a layout divided up yet connected through quiet, winding pathways. The works of art by scholars of the past dynasties such as inscribed tablets, literary couplets, poems, paintings, stone engravings, along with antique furniture and interior decorations and architectural ornamentation, reinforce people's comprehension of the landscape.

The hundred-year-old trees that make the gardens truly classical are most valuable presence in the classical gardens.

The concept and techniques of the classical gardens were introduced to Japan and Europe in the ancient times. In the 18th century, when Sir William Chambers, an Englishman, returned to England from residence in China, wrote a book on Chinese gardens, which subsequently stirred up the fervor for "Anglo-Chinese gardens" in England and Europe.

The classical garden seeks to condense the natural landscape in a limited area. Literary writers like to compare Suzhou gardens to a beautifully illustrated folding fan. Suzhou folks have the custom to adorn their courtyards with potted landscapes decorated with green moss, grass, and tiny terra cotta pavilions, terraces, bridges, and boats - even more miniaturized gardens at home.

Suzhou folks know how to enjoy life, and their interest in building gardens is truly the best dreams for the paradise of man.

The Humble Administrator's Garden is one of the most famous gardens in China, which features expansive water space dotted with isles and bridges of low railings and buildings on the water's edge, presenting a similar scene of the southern Yangtze delta.

The Surging Waves Pavilion of the Song Dy-

nasty is the oldest garden in Suzhou. For the dozen famous Suzhou gardens, we can mention the Master-of-Nets Garden, the Lingering Garden, the Lion Grove Garden, the Garden of Harmony, the Garden of Couple's Retreat, the Mountain Villa of Secluded Beauty, and the Garden of Herb Cultivation, etc. The

Half Garden is the smallest of all, but most delicate in its half scale, in which each of the pavilions, terraces, towers is built only by half, and its sparse pool is spanned by bridges only few steps long.

Listed as World Cultural Heritage by the United Nations are: the Humble Administrator's Garden the Lingering Garden, the Master-of-Nets Garden, the Mountain Villa of Secluded Beauty, the Surging Waves Pavilion, the Lion Grove Garden, the Garden of Herb Cultivation, the Garden of Couple's Retreat, and the Garden of Meditation.

The gardens will leave us a lasting memory activated by this album, to which we shall constantly come back even in our dreams.

2. 荷风四面亭。
2.The Lotus Pavilion.

3. 别有洞天。
3. Another Wonderland.

4. 塔影亭。
4.The Pavilion of Pagoda's Reflection.

5. 园林厅堂。
5.A hall inside the garden.

6. 世界文化遗产，拙政园。
6.The Humble Administrator's Garden, on the UN list of World Cultural Heritage.

7. 邻水长廊。
7. The waterside corridor.

8. 香洲残雪。
8. The Fragrant Isle in snow.

9. 见山楼雾景。
9. The Mountain-viewing Chamber in mist.

10. 秋染待霜亭。
10. The Frost-awaiting Pavilion in autumn.

11. 宜两亭春色。
11. The Pavilion of Shared Scenery in spring.

11

12. 晨雾。
12. In morning haze.

13. 涵碧山房。
13. The Mountain House of Green Waters.

14. 冬雪。

14. A snow scene.

15. 冠云峰，江南湖石假山三冠之一。

15. The Cloud-crowned Peak, the first of the top three Taihu rocks in the southern Yangtze delta.

16. 五峰仙馆。
16. The Hall of Five Fairy Peaks.

17. 鸳鸯厅扇木雕。
17. The woodwork on the partition windows of the Mandarin-ducks Hall.

18. 瑞云峰，江南湖石假山三冠之二。
18. The Auspicious Cloud Peak, the second of the top three Taihu rocks in the southern Yangtze delta.

19. 月到风来亭。
19. The Pavilion of Moonlit Night.

20. 世界文化遗产—网师园。
20. The Master-of-nets Garden, on the UN list of World Cultural Heritag.

21

21. 梯云室。
21. The Hall of Cloud-shaped Stairway.

22. 窗景
22. Picture window.

23. 园林铺地艺术。
23. The art of mosaic paving in the garden.

24. 瑞雪裹庭院。
24. The garden after smowfall.

25. 世界文化遗产——狮子林。
25. The Lion Grove Garden, on the UN list of World Cultural Heritage.

26. 假山林立。
26. A forest of peaks.

27. 湖心亭。
27. Mid-lake pavilion.

28. 秋。
28. The autumn.

29. 柳暗花明。
29. The scene brightens up inside the moon-gate.

29

30. 春雨。
30. Shizilin (Lion Forest) on a rainy day.

31. 世界文化遗产——艺圃。
31. The Garden of Herb Cultivation, on the UN list
of World Cultural Heritage.

32. 荷花小品。
32. The lotus flower.

33. 世界文化遗产——环秀山庄。
33. The Mountain Villa of Secluded Beauty, on the UN list
of World Cultural Heritage.

34. 世界文化遗产——耦园。
34. The Garden of Couple's Retreat, on the UN list of World
Cultural Heritage.

35. 隔峰窥镜湖。
35. The Mirror Lake viewed across the mountain.

36. 世界文化遗产——沧浪亭。

36. The Surging Waves, on the UN list of World Cultural Heritage.

37. 世界文化遗产——退思园。

37. The Garden of Meditation, on the UN list of World Cultural Heritage.

38. 新近建成的私家园林——翠园。

38. Cui(Jadeite) Garden a recently completed priated private garden.

苏州古城区
The Old City Proper

苏州建城已有 2515 年的历史，而且它的城垣范围和位置基本未动，这是世所罕见的。

这样的城市本身就是件收藏品。古董总是深藏的，甚至其貌不扬；而未识此宝者以为破旧一堆。其实，苏州沉淀的历史又厚又重，古巷里遍地碎石就能榨出油来，这就是苏州的文化和艺术。

一段段城墙、残缺的城门、或是修复了的城楼，真能唤起人们的历史文明感。而整个城市建设，早在宋代(公元1229年)就刻有一块石碑，称《平江图》，实际上是一幅古代的苏州地图(苏州古称平江)。整个城市的河道和街巷十分整齐地被划成棋盘格局 水陆相随，河街平行；家家户户前门是街，后门是河。生活离不开小河、船、桥。随着社会的进步，道路拓宽，城市风貌略有改变以外，那种水城古老的局面在古城区内还有所保存，还能见到一千多年前的城市格局。古代城市建设得如此科学、整齐，有远见，实用，大概在世界城市中也算少有的。在中国只有古都西安、北京是按棋盘格局规划建设的。

苏州人自己说：苏州没有小巷就不成苏州。难道风光全在小巷里?

幽雅、古朴的小巷，粉墙黛瓦，与绿水小河并行。深巷里虽然少了卖花声，却仍然传来阵阵清香，那是垂挂在深宅高墙上的藤蔓，或是跨着巷道的木香、紫藤棚。矮踏门厢房里，绣品还在绷架上，少女却打着伞出门去，一头乌发，明眸皓齿，没有艳丽花俏的服饰，却似小巷那样素净、纯清、优雅。

39

在老屋里还不时见到古树，而树龄不亚于巷口古井栏圈上深深的绳沟。

在小巷里悠转，推开普通的石库门，穿过幽暗的长弄，豁然开朗的却是座园林!

石拱桥、石梁桥、河埠，还是随处可见。它和这里的小巷一样，都有一个好听的名称，或者深藏一段神秘的故事。站在桥上或街巷口抬头仰望就是古塔。这座城市在古代就建起了高楼大厦，以至令人不可思议的是：没有水泥、钢筋、起重设备等，古代人怎么建起宏伟高大建筑物的——古塔!

现代大街建筑也是黑白灰的色调，和小巷保持一致。这好象是公认的古城特有的色调。建筑立面有起有伏，即使被遮挡在行道树间，也是那么夺目。如在雨中，那还是一幅水气淋淋的水墨写意画呢。

城里有些大街树木长得象绿荫隧道似的，快慢车道、人行道都有绿荫庇护。

触摸一下古城墙、石碑以及名胜古迹，感受一回古典园林的意境；踏勘一下小巷人家、老树古井；游荡于小船里的春风，掬捧一下小河流水；静听昆曲评弹的音调 观赏一下吴门画派的古画和精雅的苏绣；品尝苏式菜肴和糕点，醉眠天堂的梦幻，所有这些都能给人以清雅而温馨的喜悦，以至令人爱它，甚至包括它的瑕疵。无怪乎，古代意大利人马可·波罗写的世界奇书—《东方见闻录》里盛赞苏州一大城也。

在古城区里找寻的是文化历史韵味，而在城的东西两侧的工业园区和新区，则现代派十足，那是开阔胸怀，昂扬奋进的现代生活雏形。

39. 虎丘远眺。
39. A distant view of the Tiger Hill.

40. 名胜虎丘雪景。
40. The snow scene of the Tiger Hill, a famous place of historical interest.

41

2,515 years have elapsed since the founding of Suzhou City, and the city has always remained basically on the same site. That's something very rare in the world.

Such a city is worth preserving like a piece of antique, whose value is not apparent, but inherent in the eyes of the connoisseur. The historical remains of Suzhou have been so richly accumulated here that even from the stone fragments in the old alleys can cream be extracted to tell of culture and art.

A sense of history and civilization is aroused from section after section of the city wall, the dilapidated city gates, or the repaired city gate towers. The scale of urban construction can be seen from Pingjiang Map engraved on a stone stele in the Song Dynasty (1229 AD), which is the map of Suzhou, then known as Pingjiang, showing the canals, streets, and alleys laid out regularly like a chessboard. The streets and alleys extend in parallel with canals, and the houses face streets in front and lean on canals in the rear. Canals, boats, and bridges are indispensable elements in life here. With social progress, the streets are widened and the city's layout is changed to some extent. But the general form of the city on canals as was seen a thousand years ago is preserved largely within the old city proper. Perhaps few cities in the world are built with such rational, neat, lasting, and practical results. The same chessboard layout of the Chinese city can only be found in the ancient capitals of Beijing and Xi'an.

The natives say that Suzhou would be totally different without small alleys. Does that mean that all the sights are crammed inside the alleys?

In the quaint old alleys with white walls and dark roof-tiles along small canals, where flower girls seldom tread, float wisps of sweet scent from creeping ivy on tall walls of courtyard houses, or from the banksia rose or wisteria on the trellis over the pathways. Inside the one-story house and behind the waist-high door panel, an embroidery frame is still there, but the girl has gone out with an umbrella, dark hair, radiant eyes, and snowy teeth, no fancy clothes, but in simple and pure grace. In the old houses, are often seen aged trees, older than the worn-out rings of the ancient wells at the end of the alleys.

42

Down the narrow alley, behind the granite framed gate, and through the dim veranda, a classical garden would miraculously jump in sight!

Stone arch bridges, stone slab bridges, river quays are seen everywhere. Like the small alleys, they have fine-sounding names or mysterious stories. Looking up from the bridges or crossroads, you will invariably see ancient pagodas, the majestic high-rise buildings constructed in the olden times incredibly without cement, steel, and cranes.

Buildings in the modern streets also assume the tone of black, white, and grey, corresponding to those in the alleys - the tints peculiar to the ancient city. The facade of undulating buildings stands out even in the shade of trees by the sidewalks. In rain they look like paintings in fresh ink wash.

Some streets in town are so heavily shaded by trees lining both sides that the vehicle lanes seem to nestle in green tunnels.

Just touch the ancient city wall, the stone tablets, and other historical relics, and contemplate the philosophy of the classical gardens. Take a stroll down the small alleys and explore the homes and observe the aged trees and wells. Take a boat ride on the canals in spring breeze, and feel the water with your hands. Enjoy the mellow tunes of Kunqu Opera and Suzhou Ballad Singing, and marvel at the antique paintings of Wu School and the delicate Suzhou embroidery. Or taste the Suzhou-style cuisine and pastry, and drink for the dream of paradise. All these will give you a sense of intimacy and joy and inspire your love and even a charitable view of her defects. Small wonder that the good old Marco Polo, in his monumental work Oriental Sketches, lauded about Suzhou as a great metropolis.

Whereas cultural and historical flavour lingers in the old city proper, there have sprung on the flanks of the city two aspiring zones: Suzhou New District and Suzhou Industrial Park, which are advancing towards modern life with vigor and vitality.

41. 夕照吴门桥。
41. Wumen Bridge in the setting sun.

42. 苏派盆景。
42. The Suzhou-style potted plants.

43. 古盘门——全国唯一保存完好的水陆城门、始建于战国时期。

43. The ancient Panmen Gate, the only well-preserved city gate in China with both land and water gates, first built in the Warring States Period.

44

47

44. 双塔。
44. The Twin Pagodas.

45. 北寺塔、始建于明代的著名宝塔。
45. The well-known North Temple Pagoda, first constructed in the Ming Dynasty.

46. 古城鸟瞰。

46.A bird's-eye view of the ancient city.

47. 宝带桥晚霞。

47.Silhouette of the Precious Belt Bridge at dusk.

47

48. 铁铃关——明代抵御倭寇的建筑。
48.The Iron Bell Pass, a fortress against pirates during the Ming Dynasty.

49. 普济桥。
49.Puji Bridge.

50

51

50. 姑苏园。
50.Gusu Garden.

51. 玄妙观。
51.The Taoist Temple of Mystery.

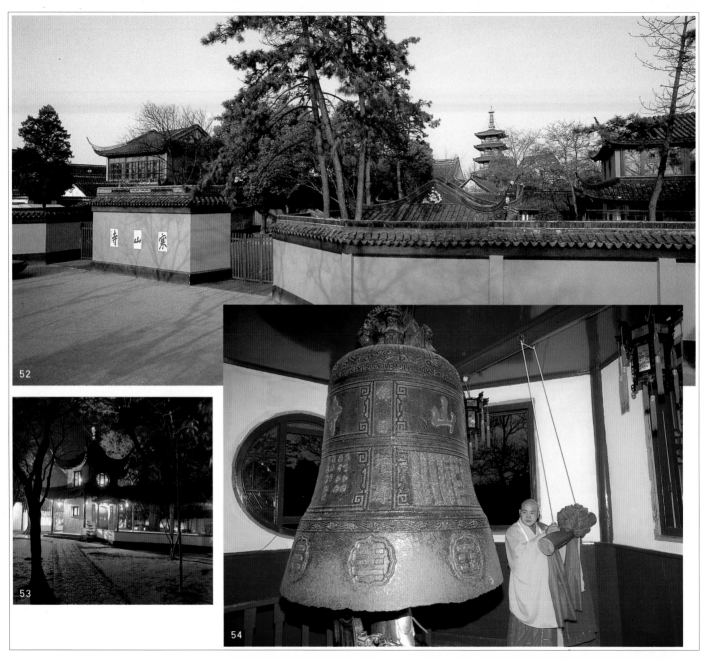

52. 寒山寺。
52.Han Shan Temple.

53. 钟楼夜色。
53.The bell tower at night.

54. 寒山钟声。
54.Bell tolling in the Hanshan Temple.

55. 通关桥水巷。
55.Tongguan Bridge over a small canal.

55

56

57

43

58. 冬练。
58.Morning exercises in winter.

63. 古戏楼台、昆曲悠悠。
63.Kunqu Opera on classical stage.

64

65

64. 鸟语。
64.The chirping birds.

65. 苏州评弹。
65.Suzhou Ballad Singing.

68. 桃花坞木刻年画。
68. Taohuawu woodblock prints of New Year pictures.

69. 苏扇。
69. Suzhou style fans.

70. 牙雕宫扇
70. An ivory fan.

71

72

71. 苏绣。
71. Suzhou embroidery.

72. 丝绸博物馆、绸庄。
72. The old fashioned silk store in Silk Museum.

77

79. 现代住宅小区。

79. A modern residential area.

80. 新区之夜。

80. Nightfall at Suzhou New District.

古 镇
Ancient Towns

正当苏州城里人面对"苏州——东方威尼斯"称号而有愧色时，郊外的几座古镇却宣扬自己是"东方小威尼斯"。

没有瑰丽的教堂，没有天顶画，没有哥特、巴洛克式的建筑，怎么是威尼斯呢?

喔! 原来古镇与威尼斯有近似的水、桥、船。

这些古镇就是由水和桥串联岛屿而成的市镇。

周庄，面积不大，却有17座石桥。人们说: 三分是水、二分是桥、剩下一半是街，这便是周庄水镇。

甪直的"甪"字，貌似古镇的地图。这里有三横三竖六条河流的走向，旧有桥梁72座半。

同里，二平方公里，有15条河流纵横，将15个岛屿由49座石桥串缀成市。

古镇比威尼斯年长资深。年长，并不等于居高临下，或昏庸、颟顸; 资深，仅仅是在历史泥路上多留下几步屐痕而已。当威尼斯人在公元413年3月25日，被北方异族驱赶到利亚尔图的地方，放下一块石块，作为一个神圣不可侵犯的避难所时，苏州附近的几座古镇已经有些来头了。

周庄，在春秋吴王时就被封为摇城; 甪直、同里早在新石器时代就有人类居住，到了唐、宋时期已成为繁荣的市镇。

甪直的保圣寺，建于梁代二年(公元503年)。罗汉塑壁，是全国文物重点保护单位。

同里古镇区基本上是明清建筑，全镇属省文物保护单位。蠡窗、砖雕门楼、宅第园

81

林有几十处。退思园、崇本堂、耕乐堂更为有名。

古镇人靠水吃饭，以至有陶器、稻谷、美术、建筑、老树，直到经济的发展。周庄在明代出了个做外贸生意的大腕，叫沈万三。他夸富到要捐钱给皇帝，犒劳军士，因而得罪了皇帝，被充军边戍而死。他留下的仅是一座沈宅和"万三蹄"一块名牌。据说，他生前将大量银子藏在一条小河中，直到现在还称为"银子浜"。而靠近沈宅的张厅，却有文人气息，另有一番景色: "轿从前门进，

船自家中过"。张厅后园的暖桥下竟然有条小河直通银子浜。

桥梁景观多多。周庄富安桥，桥身四角有桥楼，古色古香; 甪直东美桥非但桥洞由石拱砌成，连水底的桥墩也是石拱圈成; 同里的吉利桥、太平桥、长庆桥，更有风俗民情。凡家有喜事必走此三桥，祈求幸福。

河埠头是生活的倒影。姑娘们洗刷、取水，或撑船系缆，轻音笑语; 河旁的老茶馆，老人们饮茶、听书、玩鸟，恬适自在; 古镇妇女特殊的水乡服饰，色彩和谐、典雅清净，在水上船中悠然摇荡，形成图画。这里有的是流动美、色彩美、形态美，从头到脚都是美。并非夸言: 名模在此定能取得灵感。

古镇的水墙门、各式的河埠头，驳岸石刻的船扣，都显现了古代的艺术。甚至脱了榫的明式红木靠椅被冷落在天井角落里，民宅喂鸡用的钵，竟是明清时代豁了口的青花大碗……

古风神韵，无疑是古镇独有的、不需攀附旁人的、最可张扬的文化价值。

最近，中国邮政部门发行了一套包括这些水乡古镇的纪念邮票。贴一枚小小的邮票，也能让人激情飞扬，飞临水乡神游一番!

81. 夜色。
81. A night view.

56

82. 晨曲。
82. At dawn.

While the people of Suzhou are feeling a little embarrassed of the epithet Venice of the East, several ancient suburban towns are proclaiming themselves the lesser Venice of the East.

How can they call themselves Venice without splendid churches, gorgeous paintings on ceilings, or buildings of Gothic and Baroque styles?

What these ancient towns possess are the water, bridges, and boats, as Venice does!

These towns are actually isles linked up by bridges and canals.

The small town of Zhouzhuang has as many as 17 bridges. As the folks say, three tenths are water, two tenths are bridges, and the remaining half are the streets. Such is the water-bound town of Zhouzhuang.

One of the two Chinese character for the name of Luzhi Town resembles the sketch map of the town, with three canals from east to west, and three canals from south to north, at one time crossed by 72 and half bridges.

The 2-square-kilometre Tongli Town is crossed by 15 canals running through 15 isles and 49 stone bridges.

These ancient towns are senior, if not superior, to the city of Venice, in that they have left more footprints on the road of history. They have gone through ages before the Venetians were driven by the northern aliens to what is now Venice, where they laid down a stone on March 25, 413 AD to declare the place their sacred refuge.

Zhouzhuang was made the city of Yaocheng back in the time of King of Wu State in the Spring and Autumn Period. Luzhi and Tongli, evolved from human settlements of the Neolithic Age, and became thriving marketplaces in the Tang and Song Dynasties.

In Baosheng Monastery of Luzhi, built in the Liang Dynasty (503 AD), a group of clay sculptures of Buddhist Arhats is protected as a national monument.

Most of the buildings in the old part of Tongli Township date from the Ming and Qing period. The whole town is listed as a cultural relic under the protection of the provincial government. The traditional windows paneled with mica sheets, brick-carved gateways, and residential gardens can be found at sev-

83

eral dozen locations. The most famous are the Garden of Meditation, the Hall of Essential Cause, and the Hall of Happy Tillers.

Water plays a vital part in the life of the folks in the ancient towns, as seen in the craft of pottery, paddy rice cultivation, fine arts, architecture, aged trees, and the development of their economy. In the Ming

Dynasty, the merchant Shen Wansan from Zhouzhuang amassed such a great fortune that to show off his wealth he claimed to donate money to the emperor as award to army soldier of the country. The emperor felt offended and sent him on exile to the frontier, where he died. What he left behind are the House of Shens and the famous Wansan Brand Pig Leg. It is said that he used to hide his silver under a waterway, known to this day as Silver Canal. The House of Zhangs nearby is a different scene of intellectual taste: The sedan-chair enters from the front gate, and the boat passes through the house. Under the covered bridge behind the house, a small canal winds down miraculously to the Silver Canal.

The bridges afford varied scenes. Fu'an Bridge in Zhouzhuang is guarded by towers at the four corners in antique shapes. Dongmei Bridge in Luzhi is an arched stone bridge with the pier also made of a stone arch. The three bridges, Jili, Taiping, and Changqing

tening to story telling, and playing with caged birds. Peculiar to the water country is the local costume of the women in the ancient towns, in quaint and harmonious blending of colors. Their brisk movement of rowing on canals imparts a feel of beauty in colors, shapes, and movement all over. It is no exaggeration

chicken feeding is a piece of blue-and-white porcelain from the Ming.

The unique cultural value of these towns lies in the very style of antiquity in its crude and spontaneous form.

General Post Office of China recently issued a set of stamps of these ancient water-bound towns. Let the little postage stamp on the envelope trigger off your fantasy tour of the water country!

in Tongli are associated with the local customs. Whenever there is a celebration, people would pass down these bridges in pray of good luck.

The riverside is a scene of daily life, where girls do washing, fetching water, sculling or mooring their boats, or chatting. In the teahouses by the water, the senior citizens enjoy leisure hours by having tea, lis-

that even fashion models can get inspiration from the sight.

The brick watergates, quays of various shapes, carvings and boat fasteners in the stone embankment are all part of the traditional art. A broken chair deserted at the corner of a courtyard can be the mahogany chair of the Ming period, while a chipped bowl for

83. 双桥，因形同钥匙，所以又称钥匙桥。
83. The Double Bridges.

84

85

86

87

84、85、86 古宅。

84、85、86、An old-fashioned house.

87. 玉兰报春。

87. Yulan magnolia in blossom.

88. 老有所好。

88. The pastime of a senior citizen.

88

89. 水乡春早。
89. The water country in early spring.

90. 水乡游客。
90. Visitors to the water country.

91. 同里三桥。
91. The three bridges in Tongli Town.

92. 淡妆。
92. A light touch of the scene.

93. 茶楼。

93. A tea house is a place offering more than just the tea.

94. 阿婆茶。

94. The Granny's tea party.

95. 古镇晨雾。
95. The ancient town in morning mist.

95

96. 侃家常。
96. A lively chat.

97. 晨行。
97. Setting out in the morning.

99. 悉心。
99. Attentive to duty.

100. 迎春。
100. The messenger of spring.

101. 夕归。
101. Homebound at dusk.

102. 樯门内外。
102. Outside the gate.

103. 水乡婚典。
103.Wedding ceremony in the water country.

104. 掀起红盖头。
104.Unveiling the bride.

105. 新鲜事。
105. Something new.

106. 早 市。
106. At the morning market.

107

107. 老街夜曲。
107. The vibrant tune from
     an old street at night.

太　湖
Lake Taihu

太湖怎么形成的？有多种学说，其中以"海湾成湖说"为主。

太湖跨江、浙两省，是我国第三大淡水湖泊。总面积达2万4千多平方公里。

苏州处在太湖之东，所辖湖面约占总面积的七成多。

这里盛产白鱼、银鱼、梅鲚鱼和白虾、蟹以及莼菜等水生作物。

太湖盛产湖石，全是湖岸边的石灰石，经日积月累的水浪冲刷，成为皱、透、漏、瘦的精美湖石，点缀在园林里供人欣赏。

这里多岛屿和半岛，有山有水有平原，多半种植果树和茶树，有名的碧螺春茶叶就出产在这特有的湿润的小气候环境里。

这里的渔船都是五帆到七帆的大船。据说，还是宋代岳飞抗金的水兵用船，像古代兵舰似的。

这里风景如何？

写文章的人说，阿尔卑斯山有条公路，风景极佳，路边有一块牌子提示，"慢些走，欣赏！"

在苏州，沿太湖有条环太湖公路，从西山、太湖大桥，到光福、东山，宽阔的公路，一边是田野、农舍、林木；一边是芦苇、波光、白帆。不需有什么牌子，人们都会慢行、欣赏！

108

落日云霞满天，芦苇间还有野鸭随波荡漾。正当你停车取出照相机和三脚架时，芦苇丛里飞出一群野鸭，列了队似的，一任斜向天际。这是幅"落霞雁苇图"。

夜晚，皓月当空，皎洁的月光撒落在芦苇间成了碎银，那是幅"千里共婵娟"的著名摄影大师的艺术作品。

捕鱼出发时，数不清的桅杆篷帆升帐，风贯满帆，又是幅气势壮丽的千帆竞发的图画。

待到归来后，千百杆桅杆上挂满晒网，随风飘荡，延绵数里，给人悠闲、坦荡的感受，准能激发你的艺术构思。

也有人说太湖的形成是由天体落下的行星，将地球撞瘪而成的，而好奇者问：那么陨石的碎片呢？回答大概是：太湖周围都有点点山峰，从光福、胥口、藏书、木渎、东山、西山，不是都成了现在的风景区吗？

There are many theories about the formation of Lake Taihu, but the hypothesis of "sea gulf formation" has so far prevailed.

Lake Taihu, the third largest freshwater lake in China, adjoins the two provinces of Jiangsu and Zhejiang, with an area of over 24,000 square kilometres.

The city of Suzhou is situated on the east of Lake Taihu, and under its jurisdiction is over 70 % of the lake.

Lake Taihu abounds in aquatic produce such as white fish, silver fish, white anchovy, white

109

108. 归 航。
108. Back from fishing.

109. 太湖夕照。
109. Taihu Lake at srnset.

110. 晨 作。
110. The morning farm work.

110

78

shrimps, crabs, and water shields.

Plenty of Taihu rocks can be found in the lake area. Being a kind of limestone eroded by lake water for ages, the famous Taihu rocks are collected to decorate gardens. Their erect shapes are characterized by being wrinkled, pierced, slim, and naturally drained.

There are isles and peninsulas, plains and hills covered with fruit trees and tea bushes. The famous green tea, Biluochun (spring green snails), is grown in the humid climate here.

The fishing boats here are all large-sized junks with five to seven sails. It is said that they derived from the warships of ancient times, by which General Yue Fei fought the Jin invaders.

How is the scenery here?

Some writers report that along a highway in a scenic spot up in the Alps, a roadside pointer reads: "Slow down, and enjoy the sight!"

In Suzhou, a round-the-lake highway extends around Lake Taihu, passing the West Hill, Lake Taihu Bridge, Guangfu Township, and the East Hill. On one side of the road are fields, farmhouses, and tree groves, and on the other side, the reeds, glistening waves, and white sails. Without the pointer, people invariably slow down to admire the scenes!

Under the glowing sunset, wild ducks frolic in the reeds. When you pull up your car and set your camera on a tripod, a herd of wild ducks will

probably soar up in the sky, calling to mind the famous painting, "Wild Geese amidst Reeds at Sunset".

At dusk, the moonlight infiltrates the reeds in scattered silvery spots. Here we have the work by a

111

great photographic master - the moon.

When boats set out for the fishing season, we see countless masts and sails, maybe hundreds and thousands, in sheer magnitude and splendor.

After their return, fishing nets hang over the masts to dry, swaying leisurely in breeze, stretching for miles on end. This will kindle your impulse for artistic creation.

Some people say that the lake was formed after a meteorite from certain celestial body fell and hit on the earth and made a crate in the earth. Those curious might ask, "What have the scattered fragments become of?" The answer is likely to be this: "Aren't there lots of hills around the lake, now the scenic spots of Guangfu, Xukou, Cangshu, Mudu, the East Hill, and the West Hill!"

111. 早春二月。
111. The early spring.

113

112. 太湖霞光。
112. Lake Taihu aglow.

113. 石湖风情。
113. Folklore at the Stone Lake.

114. 太湖春韵。
114. Lake Taihu in vibrant spring.

115. 村 口。

115. Outside the village.

116. 渔家喜事。

116. A happy event for the fishing folks.

117. 京杭运河。

117. The Beijing-Hangzhou Grand Canal.

84

118

119

121

121. 雕花大楼，＂有江南第一楼＂之美誉。
121. The Carved Mansion, reputably "No.1 mansion in the southern Yangtze delta".

122. 东山启园。
122. Qiyuan Garden in the East Hill.

123. 石湖风光。
123. A scene of the Stone Lake.

124

124. 田 野。
124. The farmland.

125. 西山晨雾。
125. Morning fog over the West Hill.

125

126. 采枇杷。

126. Picking loquats.

127. 洞庭杨梅。

127. Bayberries in Dongting Hills.

128. 采 茶。

128. Picking the tea leaves.

129. 采红菱。

129. Gathering water caltrops.

130. 太湖秋橘。

130. Lake Taihu tangerines in autumn.

131

131. 香雪海。
131. The Sea of Snowy Fragrance.

132. 捕春风。
132. Greeted by spring breeze.

132

94

133

苏州市星级饭店
Star-rated Hotels in Suzhou

★★★★★

1. 吴宫喜来顿大酒店
电话: 0512-5103388　传真: 5100888
地址: 苏州市新市路 388 号 215007
Sheraton Suzhou Hotel and Towers
Tel:0512-5103388　Fax:5100888
388,Xingshi Rd,Suzhou,215007

2. 新苏园国际大酒店
电话: 0512-7616688　传真: 7612288
地址: 苏州市工业园区金鸡湖畔 215021
New Suzhou International Hotel
Tel:0512-7616688　Fax:7612288
Golden Rooster Lake,Suzhou Industrial
Park,Suzhou215021

★★★★

1. 竹辉饭店
电话: 0512-5205601　传真: 5208778
地址: 苏州市竹辉路 168 号 215006
Bamboo Grove Hotel
Tel:0512-5205601　Fax:5208778
168,Zhuhui Rd,Suzhou 215007

2. 雅都大酒店
电话: 0512-8291888　传真: 8291838
地址: 苏州市三香路 156 号, 215004
Suzhou Aster Hotel
Tol:0512-8291888　Fax:8291838
156,Sanxiang Rd,Suzhou 215004

3. 新城花园酒店
电话: 0512-8250228　传真: 8256258
地址: 苏州市狮山路 1 号 215011
New City Gardon Hotel
Tel:0512-8250228　Fax:8256258
1,Shishan Rd,Suzhou 215011

4. 苏州饭店
电话: 0512-5204646　传真: 5204015
地址: 苏州市十全街 115 号 215006
Suzhou Hotel
Tel:0512-5204646　Fax:5204015
115,Shiquan St.Suzhou 215006

5. 胥城大厦
电话: 0512-8286688　传真: 8271520
地址: 苏州市三香路 120 号 215004

Castle Hotel
Tel: 0512-8286688　Fax: 8271520
120,Sanxiang Rd,Suzhou 215004

6. 凯莱大酒店
电话: 0512-5218855　传真: 5218533
地址: 苏州市干将东路 535 号 215006
Gloria Plaza Hotel
Tel: 0512-5218855　Fax:5218533
535 Ganjiang East Rd,Suzhou 215006

7. 天平大酒店
电话: 0512-6268888　传真: 6267802
地址: 苏州市木渎金山路 281 号 215101
Tianping Hotel
Tel:0512-6268888　Fax:6267802
281,Jinshan Rd,Mudu,Suzhou 215101

8. 中华园大酒店
电话: 0512-6256666　传真: 6253635
地址: 苏州市木渎金山路 168 号 215101
China Garden Hotel
Tel:0512-6256666　Fax:6253635
168,Jinshan Rd,Mudu,Suzhou 215101

★★★

1. 新世纪大酒店
电话: 0512-5338888　传真: 5336798
地址: 苏州市广济路 23 号 215008
New Century Hotel
Tel:0512-5338888　Fax:5336798
23,Guangji Rd,Suzhou,215008

2. 姑苏饭店
电话: 0512-5200566　传真: 5199727
地址: 苏州市十全街相王路 5 号 215006
Gusu Hotel
Tel:0512-5200566　Fax:5199727
5 Xiangwang Rd,Shiquan St.,Suzhou,
215006

3. 乐乡饭店
电话: 0512-5222890　传真: 5244165
地址: 苏州市大井巷 18 号 215005
Lexiang Hotel
Tel:0512-5200566　Fax:5244165
16,Dajing Lane,Suzhou 215005

4. 南林饭店
电话: 0512-5194641　传真: 5193808
地址: 苏州市十全街滚绣坊 20 号 215006
Nanlin Hotel
Tel:0512-5194641　Fax:5193808

20,Gunxiu Lane,Shiquan St.Suzhou 215006

5. 乐园渡假酒店
电话: 0512-8258258　传真: 8259935
地址: 苏州市新区狮山路 108 号 215011
Amusement Land Holiday Hotel
Tel:0512-8258258　Fax:8259935
108,Shishan Rd,Suzhou New District,
Suzhou 215011

6. 国新大酒店
电话: 0512-8250188　传真: 8257031
地址: 苏州市新区狮山路 33 号
Guoxing Hotel
Tel:0512-8250188　Fax:8257031
33,Shishan Rd,Suzhou New District,Suzhou
215011

7. 园外楼饭店
电话: 0512-5331013　传真: 5334559
地址: 苏州市留园路 99 路 215008
Yuanwailou Hotel
Tel:0512-5331013　Fax:5334559
99,Liuyuan Rd,Suzhou,215008

8. 苏苑饭店
电话: 0512-5251621　传真: 5252313
地址: 苏州市东吴北路 130 号 215128
Suyuan Hotel
Tel:0512-5251621　Fax:5252313
130 Dongwu North Rd,Suzhou 215128

9. 银湖山庄　.
电话: 0512-6277888　传真: 6277888
地址: 苏州市东湖区西山太湖石公山风景区
215112
Silver Lake Villa
Tel:0512-6277888　Fax:6277888
Shigong Shan Scenic Zone,Xishan,Dongwu
District,Suzhou,215112

★★

1. 友谊宾馆
电话: 0512-5291601　传真: 5206221
地址: 苏州市竹辉路 243 号 215007
Friendship Guest House
Tel:0512-5291601　Fax:5206221
243,Zhuhui Rd,Suzhou,215007

2. 申江大酒店
电话: 0512-5331266　传真: 7232930
地址: 苏州市留园路 2 号 215008

Shenjiang Hotel
Tel: 0512-5331266　Fax: 7232930
2,Liuyuan Rd,Suzhou,215008

3. 京汇宾馆
电话: 0512-5333466　传真: 7231233
地址: 苏州市西园路 47 号 215008
Jinghui Hotel
Tel:0512-5333466　Fax:7231233
47,Xiyuan Rd,Suzhou,215008

4. 东苑宾馆
电话: 0512-7251700　传真: 7254971
地址: 苏州市干将东路 200 号 215021
Dongyuan Hotel
Tel:0512-7251700　Fax:7254971
200 Ganjiang East Rd,Suzhou,215021

5. 中山大厦
电话: 0512-7280067　传真: 7289909
地址: 苏州市人民路 559 号 215005
Zhongshan Hotel
Tel:0512-7280067　Fax:7289909
55,Renmin Rd,Suzhou 215005

6. 竹苑饭店
电话: 0512-5301641　传真: 5209971
地址: 苏州市东大街 89 号 215007
Tel:0512-5301641　Fax:5209971
89,Dongdajia St,Suzhou 215007

7. 吴中饭店
电话: 0512-5251824　传真: 5284559
地址: 苏州市吴中路 147 号 215128
Tel:0512-5251824　Fax:5284559
147,Wuzhong Rd,Suzhou 215128

★

1. 虎丘大酒店
电话: 0512-5310106　传真: 5310106
地址: 苏州市虎丘望山桥块 215008
Huqiu Hotel
Tel:0512-5310106　Fax:5310106
Wangshanqiao,Huqiu,Suzhou 215008

2. 电力宾馆
电话: 0512-6261067　传真: 6264333-2202
地址: 苏州木渎香溪东路 6 号 215101
Tel:0512-6261067　Fax:6264333-2202
6,Xiangxi East Rd,Mudu,Suzhou 215101